Waterplay

Game

About the Author

Dr. Mary Ann Humphrey is a qualified water safety instructor and has been involved in swimming activities since 1968. While instructing in the swimming program at the Sylvania Campus of Portland Community College in Portland, Oregon, she continually sought new and different ways to make swimming and water activities more fun for the students. *Waterplay* is a result of that devotion and concern.

She received her Ed.D. in teacher evaluation from the University of Northern Colorado in 1983. Many of the games and activities in this text were assessed and evaluated using this background and expertise. Presently, she is the Rock Creek Campus Coordinator of Health and Physical Education and continues to instruct in that program at Portland Community College.

The author's time is divided between teaching, writing, and sharing her home with her six-year-old son, Parke, and her longtime partner, Debra Keever. Caring for three Manx cats, a feisty cocker spaniel named Addie Rae, and a mini-lop rabbit named Jessica, adds to an active personal life.

Mary Ann Humphrey, Ed. D.
Portland Community College

Waterplay

Games and Activities for Everyone

Wm. C. Brown Publishers

Book Team

Editor *Chris Rogers*
Developmental Editor *Sue Alt*
Production Coordinator *Carla D. Arnold*

WCB Wm. C. Brown Publishers

President *G. Franklin Lewis*
Vice President, Editor-in-Chief *George Wm. Bergquist*
Vice President, Director of Production *Beverly Kolz*
Vice President, National Sales Manager *Bob McLaughlin*
Director of Marketing *Thomas E. Doran*
Marketing Communications Manager *Edward Bartell*
Marketing Manager *Kathy Law Laube*
Production Editorial Manager *Colleen A. Yonda*
Production Editorial Manager *Julie A. Kennedy*
Publishing Services Manager *Karen J. Slaght*
Manager of Visuals and Design *Faye M. Schilling*

Cover: © Mark Harmel/1989 Southern Stock Photos

Library of Congress Catalog Card Number: 88–63887

ISBN 0–697–06435–2

Printed in the United States of America by Wm. C. Brown Publishers,
2460 Kerper Boulevard, Dubuque, IA 52001

10 9 8 7 6 5 4 3 2 1

Contents

RELAY 72

Preface

In my many years of aquatic participation, I have never found a simple reference for this type of resource subject. This text is unique in that it combines many ideas from the swimming experience. Acknowledgment is given to the many students who contributed their own unique water game ideas.

Thanks are expressed to Dixie Amos, Lila Dodd, Edward Drawz, and Beth Horner for their contributions during the initial stages of the project. A special appreciation is expressed to Dr. Diane Buckiewicz for her professional comments, support and encouragement in the completion of this long awaited book.

This collection of student-originated water games and activities is offered for your enjoyment and use. Each game can be used merely for fun, the challenge of the activity, or as a way to better physical fitness through the water experience. Ideas were collected over the years from the "success" experienced by students in swim classes, aquatic game classes, and other swim-related activities. Although many tried to be creative and original, you may find similarities to old favorites. The original illustrations, by this author, have been added to help the reader better visualize each game.

This material may be used for conditioning, skill attainment, sociability, and "everyone play—everyone enjoy" concepts in aquatics. It is geared to the upper grades and older participants, and includes only those activities deemed reasonably safe or those requiring little or inexpensive equipment. All activities may be adapted to different pool sizes and arrangements. Many of the activities can also be performed by the non-swimmer. With similar adaptations, many of the games can be altered for use by special populations.

In the hope that this collection will serve a need in recreational/developmental swimming, I invite you to add your favorites to the collection by sending them to this author for future revisions. An appropriate format is supplied at the end of this text for your convenience.

Introduction

This text contains five general sections: ball, combat, miscellaneous, relay, and tag. Some sections are further divided into more specific areas. For example, the ball section has categories for baseball, basketball, football, general ball, giant ball, soccer, volleyball, and water polo. Within each section or subsection, games and activities are arranged alphabetically to aid in quick location of a particular game.

Each game or activity first lists the following information: equipment required, number of players, type of game, and area of pool where play will take place. Then the object of the activity and directions for performing it are given. Many games also contain further information which can help the activity to be successfully implemented (e.g., specific penalties and rules, suggestions, and possible variations to the game).

You will also find all games coded in the table of contents so that each one can be readily identified as to small, large, or unlimited player participation.

Small (S):   Indicates six or less players

Large (L):   Indicates seven or more players (especially necessary in team games)

Unlimited (U):   Indicates any number of players

Most of the games work best with six or more players, but many can be altered for two or three, especially in the timed or single skill activities.

Equipment

The following list has been made to help explain the general use of the equipment needed in this collection of games. It is not intended to decrease any inventive methods you may find for other uses of the described equipment.

It is hoped that these definitions will guide you in discovering new and exciting ways of using the many objects found in so many recreational pool settings.

BALLS (round)

Small:	Held in one hand, e.g., tennis ball, racquetball, Ping-Pong ball, whiffle ball, softball
Medium:	Held in one hand or both hands, e.g, rubber playground ball, rhythmic gymnastics ball, water polo ball
Large:	As above, e.g., basketball, beach ball
Super large:	Crab soccer ball, "earth" ball, giant ball

BALLS (miscellaneous)

Football, volleyball

FLOATABLE OBJECTS

Inner tubes:	All sizes can be used; can be ordered with valve stems placed on the outer surface of tube; giant tube is generally a large truck tube
Kickboards:	Floatable object used for swimming stroke improvement; made of styrofoam material, usually rectangular in shape, comes in several colors; also called flutterboard
Kicking floats:	Floatable object used to improve stroking; held between legs; also called float buoy or pullbuoy
Plastic bottles:	Empty bleach or powder bottles; also called jugs
Miscellaneous:	Any object that floats and can hold a player up may be used in place of the above mentioned objects

MISCELLANEOUS OBJECTS

Balloons:	All shapes and sizes can be used; smaller round ones work best in most balloon games
Buckets:	Refers to container for a particular goal area; waste basket can be used
Frisbees:	Used for throwing, comes in various sizes and colors; usually made from plastic

Goal area:	Can be water-basketball baskets, chair with kickboard, water polo goal cage, or other designated objects
Hand paddles:	Made of plastic, rectangular in shape, held in place by rubber straps
Leg ties:	Used to keep two players together; can be made from circular cuts of an inner tube
Mats:	Nonslip rugs used for base in some ball games; players stand on surface
Swim fins:	Used for propulsion; can also be used as sinkable object
Swim goggles:	Can also be taped for "blind" games
Swim masks:	Can also be taped for "blind" games
Team hats:	Used to designate one team from the other; water polo hats or swim caps can be used
Whiffle bats:	Used in hitting games; made of flexible, light plastic; shaped like a regular bat
Miscellaneous:	Any item not specifically identified in this section has been left out as its name is self-explanatory to its general use

POOL AREA

Deep:	An area generally used for diving or depth-type swimming activities; safe for all types of diving
Shallow:	An area used for swimming instruction that can be from waist deep to chest deep

SINKABLE OBJECTS

Diving bricks:	Used in water safety and lifesaving classes; made of solid rubber, usually black and weighing five to ten pounds; can have adhesive tape added for nonslip grip.
Diving rings:	Round rubber donuts, light weight, come in various colors
Hockey pucks:	Made of solid black rubber
Tennis shoes:	As the name implies
Weight belts:	Same as those used by divers; five, ten, or fifteen pounds; should have a buckle for easy on/off use
Miscellaneous:	Any object that will sink readily can often be used in place of the above-mentioned items

Ball

Alaska Waterball

Equipment:	Whiffle bat and ball	Type:	Ball—baseball
Player N:	2 equal teams	Area:	Shallow pool

Object To get as many points as possible. The team with the most points wins the game.

Directions Team A is in one half of the pool, team B is in the other half.

Each team takes turns at bat while the other team is outfielding until every member of both teams has had a chance to be up to bat.

The team up to bat will be in a straight line. After the batter has hit the ball *over the center line,* batter must swim around teammates; for each lap swum, a point is scored.

After a player has batted, a member of the other team picks up the ball and everyone on this team forms a straight line. The first member in line passes the ball over the head backwards and the second person passes it between the legs to the third member and so on until the ball has reached the last member of that team.

When the ball has finished being passed, the swimmer on the other team must stop. That team will be awarded as many points as laps completed.

Now the teams switch and the team that was up to bat is outfielding. This goes on until every member of both teams has been up to bat.

Variations Related game: see Ball—general—Around and Under.

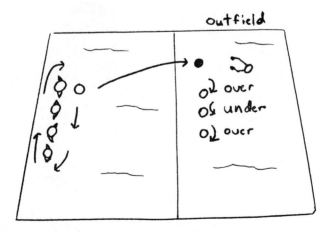

Two Pitch Ball

Equipment:	Whiffle bat and ball	Type:	Ball—baseball
	Home base mat	Area:	Shallow pool
Player N:	2 teams of 5		

Object To score runs as in softball with the following adaptations.

Directions Regular baseball rules except the following:

1. Team up to bat supplies pitcher.
2. Batter has *two* pitches to hit a fair ball. If batter does not hit a fair ball, an out is awarded.
3. No stealing.
4. Person on base cannot leave base until ball leaves pitcher's hand.
5. No bunting—batter has to take full swing.
6. People on base cannot touch ball or interfere with fielders. Penalty—out.
7. Fielders cannot interfere with swimmers unless going after ball.
8. Ball going outside pool water on fly is automatic out.
9. Players move from base to base by swimming or running.

Scoring Play five innings. One point is given for every person touching home plate after run. Play three outs or five runs per time at bat.

Variation Work-up. See Ball—baseball—water baseball

Water Baseball

Equipment: Whiffle bat and ball   Type: Ball—baseball
                Home base mat

Area: Shallow pool

Player N: 8 or more per team

Object   To make more runs than opponents.

Directions   Game is similar in manner to regular baseball. Three players in the "field" are bases, no player to mark home base needed. Each must be stationary with legs apart. One player is the pitcher. A large nonslip mat is on the deck and is used as batter's box and home. All other team members are fielders. These players help in making tag-outs.

If batter hits the ball, batter dives into the water and under the legs of each successive "base" until ball is returned to playing area. Runner is safe if through legs of base. Runner must hold onto base (shoulder) until next hit, then can proceed as far as possible without being put out.

To be put out, runner must be touched with ball on way to base or before getting through legs of base. Three outs and the batting side goes to field.

Team with the most runs wins.

Penalty   Ball hit outside pool is automatic out.

Two strikes and batter is out (pitcher should try to let batter hit ball).

Leading off base before ball is hit is an out.

Variations   Use different kind of ball.

Move base in or out depending on player's abilities.

See Ball—baseball—Two Pitch Ball.

Have Tube, Will Travel

Equipment:	Volleyball	Type:	Ball—basketball
	2 basketball goals	Area:	Deep pool
	Team hats		
	Inner tubes for each player		

Player N: 2 teams of 5 or more

Object   To score by shooting ball through opponents' basket and to keep opponents from scoring in own basket.

Directions   Suggested team is made up of two offense—*must sit* in inner tube, two defense—must be inside inner tube (may put arm inside tube), and one free person—swims free of tube.

Rules   Defense may not cross middle of pool.

Offense may not shoot unless sitting in inner tube.

Anyone may stop anyone else by holding or upsetting them out of their inner tube.

Ball out-of-bounds is put back into play by opposite team.

No one may touch the sides of the pool while participating in the game.

The free person has a duty to protect the offense while shooting, but may not shoot. The free person may also help own defense if they need help.

Variation   May eliminate free person to help control rough play.

Inner Tube Basketball

Equipment:	Inner tubes and swim fins for all 2 basketball goals Ball Team hats	Type:	Ball—basketball
		Area:	Shallow or deep pool

Player N: 2 teams of 5

Object   To score by shooting ball through opponents' basket.

Directions   Players must sit on inner tubes (fifteen-second penalty for tipping anyone over the tubes*). Ball is advanced by (1) placing it in lap and propelling tube and (2) handing it to other players. The ball may *not* be passed.

Players may shoot only in half-court; no full-court shots.

Anything goes to stop the shot except tipping the person who is shooting.

Referee determines if penalty is necessary.

Penalty   Referee may pull out player for one to two minutes if penalty time is not taken.

Referee may determine if penalty is necessary.

*Penalty time spent on deck, out of play.

Parquet Polo

Equipment: 2 basketball goals
Ball
Pullbuoy float or kickboard
   for each player
Team hats

Type: Ball—basketball

Area: Deep pool

Player N: 2 teams of at least 4

Object   To be the first team to make five baskets.

Directions   Holding the ball is allowed only while stopped in the water to shoot or to pass to another player.

Player may move with the ball only by pushing it or tapping it with the hands and arms while swimming.

Use of the legs is prohibited. Legs are to hold the pullbuoy floats or straddle the kickboards.

If a player with ball is dunked, player must let go of ball or it automatically passes to the other team.

Touch It — Shoot

Equipment:	2 basketball goals	Type:	Ball—basketball
	Ball	Area:	Shallow pool
	Team hats		

Player N: Unlimited

Object   To score more goals than the opponent.

Directions   Each team begins on the sidewall opposite the baskets. The ball is thrown into the center of the pool. Each team tries to retrieve it and have every team member touch the ball before a basket can be attempted. A fifteen-minute time limit governs the game. Players loudly number off as ball is touched.

Penalty   A free shot is given for holding or climbing onto the sides of the pool to block a shot.

Fleetball

Equipment:	2 goals	Type:	Ball—football
	Inner tube for each player	Area:	Shallow pool
	Football		
	Team hats		

Player N: 8 or more per team

Object   To score touchdown as in football.

Directions   All players are in inner tubes in teams. There is no line of scrimmage. The quarterback passes the ball to any player on the team; passing and moving the ball continues until a player with the ball is touched by an opponent.

Each team gets four downs in an attempt to get the ball into the goal area.

Only when a player has the ball can an opponent tip over the inner tube. At that point the opponents become the offense.

The game is played to a set time limit. Each goal counts one point.

Penalty   If a player is tipped while not in possession of the ball, yardage against the defense is given. The distance can be from five feet to ten feet per penalty.

Aquaball

Equipment:	2 chairs 2 kickboards Ball Team hats	Type:	Ball—general
		Area:	Shallow or deep pool

Player N: 2 teams of at least 4

Object To knock opponents' kickboard down by striking with thrown ball. Chairs and kickboards should be set in from pool edge approximately 1 1/2 feet.

Directions Game is begun with teams lined up on their own goal line. Ball is tossed into center upon signal to begin play.

Ball may be played according to swim ability of players. For example, beginners may throw or swim ball to advance but *no* personal contact allowed. More advanced players may throw or swim ball to advance and ball may be taken from a player providing no personal roughness. May allow dunking if group is agreeable.

Score is made when ball strikes board on the fly and tips it over. A deflected strike (from deck or wall, etc.) is no score.

Out-of-bounds ball is put back in play at that spot by a player of the team not causing out-of-bounds.

Only the goalie may hold the goal line gutter for playing advantage.

After score, defending goalie puts ball back into play as quickly as possible.

Suggestions Played in deep water: provides an excellent conditioner.

Played in shallow water: any skill level is able to participate.

Around and Under

Equipment:	Ball (softball size)	Type:	Ball—general
Player N:	Unlimited	Area:	Shallow pool

Object To complete course before other team can retrieve ball and finish their course.

Directions Two teams organize at opposite ends of the pool. One forms a line across the width, the other is in scattered position at the other end.

The first person in the "line" team tosses the ball at the other team. The line player then immediately tries to swim around the entire line of players.

The retrieving team forms a column and passes the ball underwater between the legs of each player from one end to the other and back again.

If the throwing side completes task first, a point is scored; if the retrieving side is first, one out is scored against the throwing side (i.e., like baseball). After three outs the retrieving team is "up". ("Up" team takes turns as to who throws ball.)

Variation May alter the number of times a swimmer goes around line depending on number of players and skill level.

Beach Ball Dodgeball

Equipment: Beach balls   Type: Ball—general

Player N: Unlimited   Area: Deep pool

Object   To avoid being hit with the ball.

Directions Use dodgeball rules with one or two beach balls.

Feet Ball

Equipment:	Goal markers (chairs)	Type:	Ball—general
	Ball		
	Inner tubes for each player	Area:	Shallow or deep pool

Player N: 2 teams of at least 4

Object   To move the ball through the opposing team's goal with the feet to score a point.

Directions   Each person will sit in an inner tube. Arms and legs may be used for propulsion.

Play is started when each team is touching their side of the pool. The referee throws the ball into the middle.

Ball may be passed to teammates through the air, but as soon as it touches the water, it must be picked up with the feet.

If a player falls out of tube or is dumped, that player must get back into the tube in a sitting position *before* either touching the ball or resuming play.

Rules   The ball cannot be touched with anything but feet when it is in the water. The goalie is the only one who may pick up the ball from the water with hands.

A person may be dumped from tube *only* when holding ball. This includes goalie.

The ball may be touched or played only by someone sitting in an inner tube.

Only the goalie and the person with the ball may be behind the goal lines.

Penalties   If any of the first three rules are broken, a penalty will be called by the referee. The violator will go straight to the penalty box and the teams will resume same positions as at the beginning of the game. The referee will resume the game by throwing the ball into the middle of the pool. Violator remains in the penalty box for one scoring period and then returns to game.

The referee reserves the right to call a foul on anyone who breaks the last rule and may impose the same penalty as above.

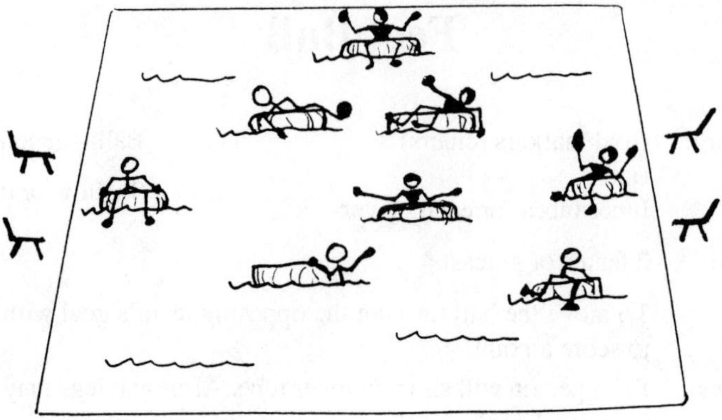

Flip Flop

Equipment: Goal markers
                  Pair of fins for each player
                  Medium ball
                  Team hats

Type: Ball—general

Area: Shallow pool

Player N: Unlimited

Object   To flip ball with fins into opposing team's goal.

Directions   Divide pool in half. Game can be played by length or width. Designate a goal area for each team. Game is played by moving ball only with fins. Use of hands is not allowed. Ball is flipped into goal area with fins. Begin game with each team on opposing sides. Toss ball into center.

Can be played to points or a time limit and points.

Penalty   For use of hands, a free kick at the goal is given the opposing team. Kicker must be five feet from goal.

Fluctuatnechmergitar
"Fluc tu Wat"

Equipment:	2 medium balls	Type:	Ball—general
Player N:	4 or more per team	Area:	Deep pool

Object   To be the team that keeps ball in the air the longest.

Directions   Form two circles and begin tossing the ball rapidly from player to player. If a player drops the ball or goes underwater, that player is out.

The game is played to a time limit; the team having the most players left is the winner.

Hands Aweigh

Equipment:	Large beach ball (3′ diameter)	Type:	Ball—general
	2 3′ × 4′ pieces of plastic sheeting with a black X prominently marked*	Area:	Shallow pool
	Team hats		

Player N: 2 teams of 2 to 8

Object

To touch the opponents' end wall of the pool with the ball or—for more points—the black X on the piece of plastic.

Directions

Play is begun by placing ball in middle of pool while each team is lined up on opposite pool sides.

Hands and arms may not touch ball. Ball is pushed and touched with feet, shoulders, head; it may even be blown.

Three points are made by the team that touches opponents' wall with the ball. Ten points are scored if a team touches the X on the opponents' plastic sheet with the ball.

Game may be timed or total points scored, whichever comes first.

Rules and Penalties

If a player touches the ball with the hand or arm, a foul has been made. The offending player sits out of the game for one minute while the remaining players continue play.

*Each plastic sheet with an X is placed on either side (or end) of the pool, hanging over the edge and weighted at the top.

Hot Ball

Equipment:	Ball	Type:	Ball—general
	Stopwatch		
	Scorekeeper/referee	Area:	Shallow pool
	Team hats		

Player N: Unlimited

Object   To have the ball in team's possession when time limit ends.

Directions   Teams are lined up on opposite sides of the pool. The ball is tossed into the center by the scorekeeper/referee. Each play is governed by a two-minute time limit; twelve minutes in a period. During that time team members must move the ball— similar to "keep away"—from player to player. At the end of each two-minute time limit, the team with the ball receives two points. The team with the most points at the end of the period wins.

The ball is passed with one hand but may be caught with two.

A player may not hold the ball longer than ten seconds.

Penalty   A player must sit out for thirty seconds if a foul is committed.

Variations   Change time limit.

Change tossed object (smaller ball, ring, etc.).

Play to music; when music stops, score possession. Team in possession loses points.

Hot Ball Pass

Equipment:	Ball (medium size)	Type:	Ball—general
Player N:	Unlimited	Area:	Deep pool

Object To be the last remaining player not to drop the passed ball.

Directions Start in a large circle. The ball is continually passed in the air from player to player while all tread water.

Each player who drops the ball is out of the game.

Game is played until only one player remains.

Variations Vary size of ball.

Play in teams, moving the ball quickly, counting number of passes.

Number of passes, player number, and a time limit are further variations.

Name Toss

Equipment:	Ball	Type:	Ball—general
Player N:	5 or more	Area:	Shallow or deep pool

Object   To learn the names of other swimmers, to facilitate further game action, and to get acquainted with one another.

Directions   Players are arranged in a circle.

Name of recipient is called out and ball tossed high in air to that person; recipient should catch it before it strikes the water (beginners—in shallow water, standing depth; more advanced—in deep water, treading).

Suggestions   It is helpful if players are not allowed to throw to adjacent people.

For large groups, split into several small circles of five to seven players. Gradually combine circles.

With increase of skill and knowledge, two balls may be used.

Poison Ball

Equipment:	Waterpolo ball	Type:	Ball—general (combat)
Player N:	Unlimited	Area:	Shallow or deep pool

Object   Eliminate players by having the ball touch the player.

Directions   Form a circle with all players. A ball is placed in the center. All players try to work others in the circle toward the ball. All must hold hands. When a player is touched by the ball, that player is eliminated. The final player untouched by ball is the winner.

Scramble Ball

Equipment:	15 or more balls	Type:	Ball—general
Player N:	10 or more	Area:	Shallow or deep pool

Object   To retrieve as many balls as possible and return to home base.

Directions   Place all the balls in the center of the pool. Teams line up on opposite sides. On the signal, both teams swim to the balls, trying to retrieve as many as possible and swim to the opposite side. As the players pass, opposing members try to knock loose balls and retrieve for their own side.

Variation   Change size of ball.

Tube Ball

Equipment:	4 inner tubes anchored to pool bottom Ball Chalkboard and chalk for scoring	Type:	Ball—general
		Area:	Deep or shallow pool

Player N: 2 or 3 teams of at least 2

Object Players try to throw ball into opponents' inner tubes to score points against them.

Directions Ball is thrown into center of pool. Teams swim from sides of pool to ball. Two of the tubes should be designated as "extra" when only two teams are playing. Players try to throw ball into opponents' designated tube to score points against team. Can be played to a set time limit.

Scoring Team with lowest number of points against them wins the game. A team has a point scored against it when the ball enters its tube. Any team placing ball in extra tube can choose to subtract a point from their score *or* add a point to each of the other teams' scores.

Rules No touching the tubes.

Only player with ball may be dunked.

Only one hand on the ball at a time (*variation:* two hands by choice of referee).

Penalty One free throw from center by each team against the team committing a foul upon rules above.

Note BEWARE! Complicated scoring.

23

Whirlball

Equipment: 2 balls   Type: Ball—general

Player N: 6 or more per team   Area: Shallow or deep pool

Object   To complete a certain number of circle revolutions with team ball.

Directions   Players form a circle with opposing players side by side so the circle is evenly mixed.

             The starters of each team begin to pass the ball from teammate to teammate. Each team must pass the ball to others on the team in succession, staying in their own positions each time. Opposing members should try to knock the ball away while still passing their own ball around.

             The retriever must return to the retriever's original spot before passing the ball on. Starters keep track of revolutions stating so out loud.

Variation   Can be played to a set limit. May have team hats on one team for easier identification.

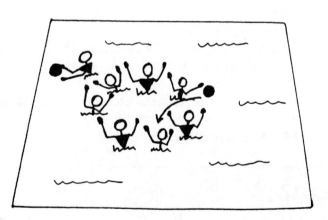

Bulldozer

Equipment:	Giant ball		Type:	Ball—giant ball
	Team hats			
	Swim fins (optional)		Area:	Deep pool

Player N: 2 teams of at least 3

Object Each team tries to push the ball to the opposite wall.

Direction Play is begun with teams lined up on opposite sides and ball is placed in the center. At the signal, both teams move out to try to push the ball to the opposite wall.

The ball is to be pushed by the head and may not be touched by the hands, feet, or any other part of the body. Swim fins may be used if swimming skill warrants it.

A point is scored each time the ball comes in contact with the goal line wall. After a score has been made, the teams again line up along their respective sides of the pool; the ball is placed in the center and play is resumed on signal.

Rules and Penalties If a person is seen by the referee to push the ball with hands or feet, that person must retire to the edge of the pool and remain out of the game until another point has been scored.

No player may hold another player underwater or in any other way harm the other player. Penalty: expulsion from game.

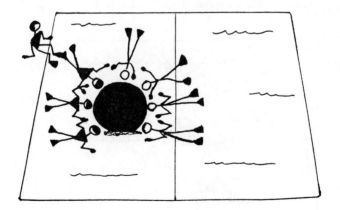

Wally Ball

Equipment:	Giant ball	Type:	Ball—giant ball

Equipment: Giant ball
Inner tube for each player
Team hats

Type: Ball—giant ball

Area: Shallow or deep pool

Player N: 2 teams of at least 3

Object   To move the giant ball to the opponents' goal.

Directions   Teams line up along their goal lines seated in inner tubes. At the signal to start, both teams race for center of pool as referee throws ball into the center. Teams attempt to move ball to opponents' goal line any way possible—throw, push, kick, etc.

Rules   If a player is flipped out of the inner tube, that player cannot touch ball or flip anyone else out of an inner tube until sitting position has been regained in tube. Ball will be turned over to opposite team if this foul is committed.

If ball is knocked out-of-bounds it goes to opposite team for throw-in.

Each team may have two time-outs of three seconds each per game.

Variations   Can be played for points or a time limit.

Ball may only be moved with the feet and legs.

May be played without inner tubes.

May place giant ball in giant inner tube.

Corner Goal

Equipment:	1 large inner tube (truck size)	Type:	Ball—soccer
	1 regular inner tube per player	Area:	Shallow pool
	Goal markers		
	Team hats		
	Ball		

Player N: 14 or more

Object   To pass the ball while in inner tube and make a goal.

Directions   Each team has the following positions: one center, one goalie, and the remaining players divided into forwards and guards.

Goalies must stay near but not in the goal area. Centers remain on large inner tube. Guards play in their own half of the pool. Forwards may move freely about, but not into the goal area.

The pool is divided diagonally. The play begins with all players in inner tubes. The ball is sent to the centers for control. Anything is allowed between forwards and guards, but nothing can be done to goalies or centers.

The ball continues in play until a goal is scored. A score brings the ball back to the opponents' center and play begins again.

Each goal scores one point. Game can be played in quarters or to a total time limit.

The team with the most points wins.

Penalty   A thirty-second penalty "sit out" is given a player for pushing or dunking a center or goalie.

Frog Soccer

Equipment:	Inner tubes for all except goalies	Type:	Ball—soccer
	Swim fins for all		
	Team hats	Area:	Shallow pool
	Ball		
	2 goal markers		

Player N: Approximately 12 or more

Object   To play ball only with the fins and to score a goal.

Directions   Game is to be played much like soccer with each team having a forward line, a back-up line, and a goalie. Goalie is to guard by holding onto or sitting on side of pool. He or she blocks and kicks with fins. Best to use tallest team member for goalie.

Use teamwork by staying in approximate area of assigned positions, blocking and passing together. Second line is to play defense only; not to pass center line of pool.

Everyone sits in inner tubes except goalies.

Play begins with referee's throw into center of pool.

Teams may tip each other over.

Rules and   Player is not to play when out of inner tube. If player is caught
Penalties   doing so or using hands, penalty is one minute out of the pool.

Goal: three points.

Head Soccer

Equipment:	2 goal markers	Type:	Ball—soccer

Equipment: 2 goal markers   Type: Ball—soccer
Ball
Team hats   Area: Shallow pool

Player N: 7 or more per team

Object   To use head to get ball into opponents' goal.

Directions Players may move in all directions. One player should be a goalie.

Ball is moved only by use of the head. If a direct hit cannot be performed, the ball may be tossed up and hit with the head. It may also be held and hit out of the hands with the head. Players may block flight of the ball with one hand only.

The team to score the most points is the winner.

Variation Play in inner tubes.

29

Super Soccer

Equipment: Goal markers or water   Type: Ball—soccer
                polo nets
              Ball   Area: Shallow or deep pool
              Team hats
              Inner tube for each player

Player N: 2 teams of at least 3

Object   To put the ball between or into the goal markers. Each goal counts as two points.

Directions   Players will divide evenly into two teams with designated colored team hats.

Each player must remain seated in inner tube at all times during the game.

Ball is advanced by throwing.

The four sides of the pool are out-of-bounds.

The first team to acquire ten points wins the game. If time runs out and neither team has the ten points, then the team with the required most points will win.

Dunking and related acts are forbidden.

Water Volleyball

Equipment:	Volleyball net Volleyball Floated rope boundaries Inner tube for each player	Type:	Ball—volleyball
		Area:	Shallow pool (preferably)

Player N: 2 teams of at least 6

Object To play volleyball in swimming pool.

Directions Net should be stretched across width of pool about 1 1/2 feet above water surface.

Players sit in inner tubes.

Volleyball rules for play except that (1) serve is thrown and (2) unlimited hits per side.

Variation Play without inner tubes.

Note Keep court area small as it is difficult to move quickly in water.

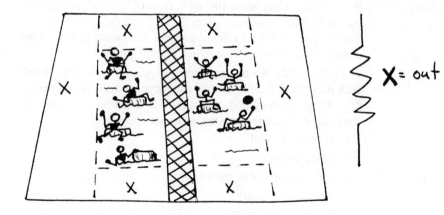

X = out

Alternate Water Polo

Equipment:	Ball	Type:	Ball—water polo

Equipment: Ball
2 goals
Team hats
Inner tubes for each player

Type: Ball—water polo

Area: Shallow or deep pool

Player N: 2 teams of at least 5

Object To score by firing the ball into the opponents' goal.

Directions The two teams consist of an equal number of players wearing hats color-keyed to their team. The goalies wear red hats. It is suggested that the teams have two forwards, one center, two defense people, and a goalie.

The game is played in four quarters. The first and third quarters are ten minutes and played in inner tubes. The second and fourth quarters are six minutes and played by the regular rules. There will be a two-minute break between quarters.

Rules Start of play: Both teams line up in front of the goal they defend. At the whistle the referee tosses the ball into the pool. From this time on there will be no time-outs until the quarter is over. After a goal, the team which was scored on will get the ball.

Playing the ball: No player except the goalie may touch the ball with two hands. No player may submerge the ball. No player except the goalie may play the ball while touching the bottom of the pool. A player is permitted to do the following:

1. Dribble the ball
2. Seize the ball
3. Lift the ball out of the water
4. Remain stationary
5. Pass or shoot the ball
6. Play the ball while it is in the air

Out of Play: The ball is out of play when it (1) hits the side of the pool, (2) lands out of the water, or (3) crosses the goal line. In the cases of (1) and (2), the ball goes to the closest opposing player; for item (3), it goes to the goalie.

Fouls It is a foul to do the following:

1. Hold the ball underwater
2. Hold the opponent underwater
3. Push off the wall

4. Punch the ball
5. Punch the opponent
6. Splash water into opponent's face
7. Jump from the floor of the pool
8. Deliberately impede an opponent unless he/she has ball
9. Touch the ball with two hands
10. Push an opponent
11. Dunk an opponent
12. Stand or walk on the floor of the pool

Penalty   All fouls will result in offended team getting the ball.

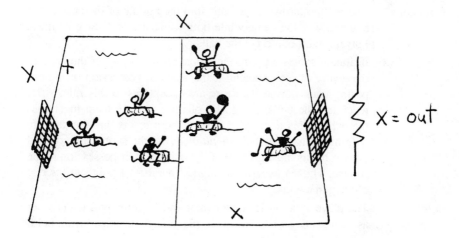

Corner Water Polo

Equipment:	3 balls	Type:	Ball—water polo
	6 kickboards		
	2 goals (chairs)	Area:	Deep pool
	2 nets behind goals		
¿	Team hats		
	2 anchored goal lines		

Player N: 2 teams of at least 5

Object To throw the ball at the goal to score a point.

Directions The referee throws three balls into the middle of the pool at the beginning of the game while both teams are on their goal lines. Players swim out to get the balls.

If a team scores a point, they must relinquish all of the balls to the goalie of the opposing team. Balls in possession of the opposing team during the score are exceptions to this rule. After receiving the balls, the goalie of the opposing team must pass the balls to his team. If players of both teams throw and score with more than one ball *simultaneously*, the scores are counted but the teams must give all of the balls in their possession to the referee. The teams with the highest number of points at the end of the game wins.

Rules The players can swim underwater and hold the ball underwater as long as they wish. However, players are forbidden from holding individuals underwater.

Only three players per team, including the goalie, can use kickboards.

No player can cross the goal lines *unless* the goalie has crossed over the goal line and is in the playing area.

If the goalie moves outside the goal territory, the opposing team can capture the goalie who *cannot* resist capture. Only members of the goalie's team can bring the goalie back to the goalie territory.

The goalie is the only player who may hold on to the sides of the pool.

Players with kickboards can swim anywhere in the playing area; they must hold on to the boards at all times if they have the ball. They can relinquish the boards to other players if they wish.

Players cannot hit individuals with the boards or block the passing of the ball with boards.

34

Players are forbidden from hitting or kicking other individuals. Penalty for fouls: (1) relinquishment of balls to opposing team or (2) the goalie of a team must swim out to playing area.

Water Croquet

Equipment:	Ball (medium)	Type:	Ball—water polo
	Large mat	Area:	Shallow pool
Player N:	8 or more per team		

Object

To score more runs than opposing team.

Directions

The team in the water assumes two kinds of positions: (1) six wickets (players stationary with legs apart) and (2) ball fetchers. The team that is up is on the deck with the first kicker standing on the large mat.

The ball is kicked and the player dives in the water, passing through as many "wicket" legs as possible before being tagged by the opponent with the retrieved ball. If the player is tagged after going under a wicket, that player must remain there until the next kick of the ball.

Players move underwater through the wickets until all on a team have kicked the ball. Then the opponents are up.

Points are scored by each player that makes the entire run either all at once or in segments. When both teams have kicked the ball, runs are added up. The team with the most runs wins.

Variation

Move the wickets for greater challenge.

W = wicket
F = Fetcher

Combat

Blind Man's Tough

Equipment: Blindfolds for bottom players   Type: Combat

Player N: Even teams of 2   Area: Shallow pool

Object   To be the last team left standing.

Directions   Divide equally into groups of two. The bottom player must wear a blindfold at all times. The second player rides on the bottom player's shoulders.

Teams begin play at opposite sides of the pool and advance to the center by directions from the shoulder player. Both the bottom and top players may try to upset their opponents.

Play continues until one team remains standing.

Note   Official should warn when player pairs get too close to edge while in combat.

Body Push

Equipment: Optional—kickboards*   Type: Combat

Player N: Unlimited   Area: Shallow or deep pool

Object To push opponent across a designated line.

Directions Two opponents face each other. They assume a "tugboat" position, clasp hands with opponent, and try to push opponent across a designated line or marker with freestyle kick.

Variations Have four people form a square all pushing opposites.

Have opponents lie on backs.

Have opponents vary type of kick used.

*Have opponents hold opposite sides of a kickboard.

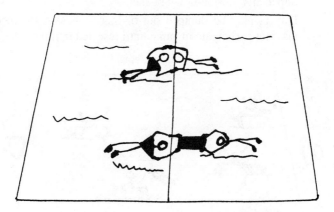

Bury the Bacon

Equipment: Towel wrapped tightly
     in tape
2 buckets
Inner tube for each player
Team hats

Type: Combat

Area: Shallow or deep pool

Player N: 2 even teams, any number

Object To bury the "bacon" totally under the bucket.

Directions Game and play-after-point begin with towel thrown into center of pool while both teams are lined up on own pool sides, sitting in inner tubes.

Towel is moved any way possible. Players try to put towel under opponents' upside-down bucket.

Players may be dumped out of inner tubes. A dumped player may not participate in game until reseated in inner tube.

Inner Tube Combat

Equipment: Inner tube for each player   Type: Combat
Team hats

Area: Shallow or deep pool

Player N: 2 teams of 4 or more

Object   Team A tries to cross pool twice seated in inner tubes while team B attempts to unseat them. In the next round, the roles are reversed.

Directions   Teams line up on opposite sides of the pool. At the whistle, team A attempts to cross the pool. Team B tries to dump them. Once a person is dumped out, that player must stay at the same spot. Each person on team A who gets back to starting line counts one team point.

After the points are tallied for team A, team B attempts to score while team A become the "dumpers."

Variation   Both teams try for points and are dumpers simultaneously.

Note   Hazards may be reduced with appropriate regulations.

Kickboard Mayhem

Equipment:	Color-coded kickboards for each player	Type:	Combat—ball
	Team hats	Area:	Shallow pool
	Medium ball		
	2 goal markers		

Player N: Unlimited

Object To cause ball to go into opponents' goal by use of the kickboard.

Directions If kickboards can be given by team color (e.g., one team has red, one team has blue) it contributes to the play. Hats should also be worn.

Mark off goal areas for each team. Ball must go through goal area in order to score. Balls going outside the area should be returned to the team that did not hit it out.

Ball is moved, trapped, pushed, smashed, or thrown by use of only the kickboard. No hands can touch the ball. Anything is allowed (e.g., swamping players, splashing water, and so on).

Players can toss the ball with kickboard by lifting and tossing forward or by a backward toss with back to goal.

Each goal counts one point. The team with the most points at the end of a time limit wins.

Penalty Ball is given to opponents when foul involving hands is called.

Variation Change size of ball.

Push-A-War

Equipment:	None	Type:	Combat
Player N:	2 teams of at least 4	Area:	Shallow pool

Object   To push opponents across designated mark.

Directions Divide into two teams and select two pushers per team. Remainder of teammates divide so that half are behind one pusher and half are behind the other.

The pushers hook inside arms. The players behind the left pusher are in a line. Each player grabs the left leg of the person in front with the right hand. Players behind the right pusher do the opposite.

At the signal the four pushers (with the teammate lines following) join outside hands in the center of the pool.

Each team acts as a unit and tries to push the other team one-fourth the distance from the center of the pool.

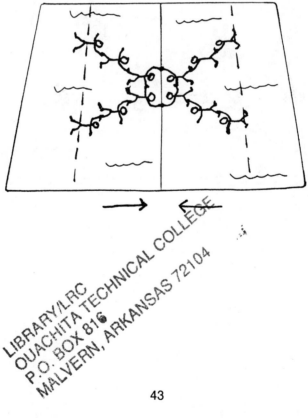

Tube Takeover

Equipment:	Inner tube for every other player Team hats	Type:	Combat
		Area:	Shallow or deep pool

Player N: 8 or more

Object   To capture all inner tubes for team.

Directions   Divide teams so that each team has half as many inner tubes as there are players. Members decide who will be in tubes for initial combat and who will wait in line for retrieved tubes.

At the command, the floating players will try to upset opponents. When a player is upset, that player must give inner tube to player in waiting opponents' line. The players without inner tubes must then wait in line for new inner tube.

A team wins when all players have possession of and are floating in an inner tube.

Tube Tug-of-War

Equipment: Cloth marker   Type: Combat

               Long rope

               Inner tubes for each player   Area: Shallow or deep pool

Player N: Unlimited

Object   To pull opponents across a designated line.

Directions   All players sit in inner tubes facing their opponents. A cloth marker should be tied at the center of the rope to indicate progress. On command, all players try to pull the opposing players across the designated mark.

Penalty   If a player falls out of the inner tube, that player cannot pull the rope until righted in the inner tube.

Variation   Players falling out of inner tubes may not return to game.

Water Tug-of-War

Equipment:	Long, thick rope Cloth marker	Type:	Combat
Player N:	2 teams of at least 3	Area:	Preferably deep pool Shallow may be used

Object
To pull opposing team across the dividing line or point.

Directions
Played as regular tug-of-war but ideally executed in deep water.

May use a painted lane line as a center point or have referee watch a specific fixed point or use cloth marker.

Note
May be more challenging for shallow water play; also, younger players may enjoy more if shallow water used.

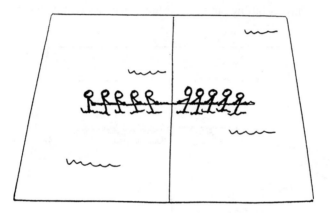

Miscellaneous

Land Adapted
Leader
New World
Special Equipment
Underwater

Musical Inner Tubes

Equipment:	1 less inner tube than players	Type:	Miscellaneous— land adapted
	Record and player or radio	Area:	Shallow or deep pool
Player N:	Unlimited		

Object To be the remaining player with inner tube when music stops.

Directions Place all inner tubes in a circle. All players continually circle the inner tubes without touching them. The music or sound is playing during this period.

The leader is on the deck and gives an unseen signal to the music operator that stops the sound.

All players rush to an empty inner tube and get in so the arms are over the top. The player without an inner tube is out of the game, and one more inner tube is removed.

Play continues until one player remains and is the winner.

Variation Adjust the distance the players are to the inner tubes as the music is playing.

48

Red Runder

Equipment: None   Type: Miscellaneous—land adapted

Player N: Unlimited   Area: Shallow pool

Object   To have land player dive in and break through pool players line.

Directions   One team stands in pool facing end with hands clasped and legs apart. The other team is on the deck. When the pool team chants "Red runder, red runder, send _____ right under," the named player dives into the pool and tries to get through the line. The swimming player must stay underwater during the attempt. If the player does not make it, that player becomes a part of the line team.

Variation   Have all the land players go into the pool at the same time.

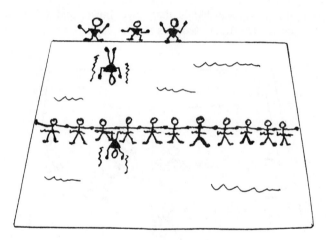

Underwater Soccer

Equipment: 1 hockey puck or 2 taped
           diving rings
           Tennis shoes for each player

Type: Miscellaneous—
          land adapted

Area: Shallow pool

Player N: 5 or more per team

Object   To score a goal with the puck by kicking it underwater.

Directions   Players move a hockey puck by kicking it with their feet. Only three kicks in a row by one member are allowed. Two opposing players face off in the center to begin the game. Each team tries to kick the puck through a designated goal at the opposing team's end of the pool once the face-off has been completed.

One point is scored per goal. Game may be played for points or time.

Penalty   If a player uses hands, that player must stand where the fouls occurred for fifteen seconds before playing again.

Alphabet Trap

Equipment:	None	Type:	Miscellaneous—leader (tag)
Player N:	Unlimited	Area:	Shallow pool

Object To avoid being tagged while swimming across pool.

Directions Select one leader to call letters of the alphabet. The remaining players are equally divided on each side of the pool with the leader in the middle.

When the leader calls out any letter of the alphabet and a player has that letter in his or her first or last name, that player must attempt to swim to the opposite side without being tagged.

If a player is tagged the player freezes in place. Only the original person can continue to move around, but the frozen players can tag while remaining in place.

The remaining free player is the winner.

Blind Battle

Equipment:	2 inner tubes	Type:	Miscellaneous—
	Blindfolds for water players		leader (combat)
	(swim goggles with tape)	Area:	Shallow pool
Player N:	Unlimited		

Object To capture opponents' "flag" without being eliminated.

Directions Each team selects a "troop commander" who remains on the deck. All water players put on blindfolds and remain in their own half of the pool until the command is given.

The inner tube is the flag for the command headquarters. Each team advances toward the opponents' flag by voice directions from the leader.

Inner tubes remain near the back side of each command post. Teammates may touch only the opponents' inner tube.

When players of opposing sides contact each other, both are eliminated from the battle. Leaders should learn names of players before battle for easier directions.

The first team to capture the flag is the winner.

Variation Play to a time limit and see which team has advanced the farthest to determine the winner.

Blindman's Basketball

Equipment:	2 basketball goals	Type:	Miscellaneous—leader
	2 medium balls	Area:	Shallow pool
	Blindfolds (taped goggles)		

Player N: Unlimited

Object   To score more baskets while blindfolded than opponents.

Directions Each team selects player that will be blindfolded. The rest of the players assist the blind player by telling the player how and where to shoot in order to make a basket. The game is played to a time limit. The team with the highest score wins.

Variations Use more than one blind shooter.

Use only one basket having all blind shooters in close position (concentration important).

Chicken Fat

Equipment:	Record—"Chicken Fat"	Type:	Miscellaneous—leader
Player N:	Unlimited	Area:	Shallow pool

Object Warm-up activity

Directions Adapt the land activities to water by following-the-leader. The "Chicken Fat" recording gives specific activity directions. It is advisable to use said music for most fun and action. Other records with similar follow-the-leader activities can also be substituted. Note: For those not familiar with the record, it is basically a directed land exercise routine that can be adapted for the water.

Jump or Dive

Equipment:	Low diving board	Type:	Miscellaneous—leader and diving
Player N:	Unlimited	Area:	Deep pool

Object To be able to perform called command while in the air.

Directions Choose one caller to give signals of "jump" or "dive." All other players line up at diving board.

As the player bounces to leave board, the caller says either "jump" or "dive." The player then tries to go in feet first (jump) or head first (dive).

The player coming closest to the called instruction is the winner.

Variations Points can be used to rate each performance.

Use "backward" or "forward" as calls (player enters water feet first but would have to twist in the air to obey command).

Ship, Dock, Lighthouse

Equipment:	Lane marker	Type:	Miscellaneous—leader
	End of pool markers	Area:	Shallow pool
Player N:	Unlimited		

Object To reach correct destination called before other players.

Directions Pool is divided into three sections. The lane marker can be attached across the middle of the pool for the dock section. Opposing ends are the ship and lighthouse, respectively.

Players begin in the middle. The caller can call any spot he or she wishes. If the spot called is ship the players swim toward that end; if lighthouse, to that end. If the caller calls the spot where the players are and someone starts to swim, that swimmer is out. The last person to arrive at a called destination is also out.

The caller may call a new location before the swimmers reach the previously called spot.

Variations Strokes used, method of going through water, and whistle blasts instead of places called are possible variations.

Water Follow the Leader

Equipment: None   Type: Miscellaneous—leader

Player N: 2 teams   Area: Shallow or deep pool
             Best with small group

Object   To imitate the water skill of opponent.

Directions   Player on team A must imitate water performance of easy skill of player on team B to earn a point for team.

Then player on team B must imitate water performance of easy skill of player on team A to earn a point for team.

Referee judges point allowance.

Corkscrew Swim

Equipment: None   Type: Miscellaneous—New World game

Player N: Unlimited   Area: Shallow or deep pool

Object   To get across the pool safely.

Directions   Swim by alternating one crawl arm pull on front, with one crawl arm pull on back.

Variation   Begin with three front crawl arm pulls and three back crawl arm pulls. Next, do two front crawl arm pulls and two back crawl arm pulls.

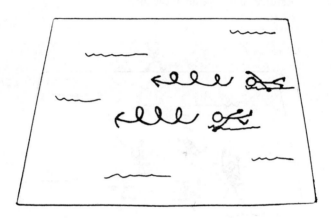

Garbage

Equipment: 15–20 floatable objects
(inner tubes, kickboards,
balls, etc.)

Type: Miscellaneous—
New World game

Area: Shallow or deep pool

Player N: 6 or more

Object   To get all objects to opponents' side.

Directions   Place all objects in center of the pool. Have all players swim to object on signal. All try to toss objects to opponents' side so that own side remains clear. First team with a clear area wins.

Note   May wish to divide pool area into two "yards" with a rope.

Frisbee Dunk

Equipment:	2 goal markers	Type:	Miscellaneous—
	Frisbee		special equipment
	Team hats	Area:	Shallow pool
Player N:	6 or more per team		

Object   To score goal by passing Frisbee and placing it in goal area.

Directions   Designate goal areas with markers. Frisbee is thrown into the center of the pool. Team members pass the disk from player to player until two players can place it by hand in opponents' goal area.

Interceptions can occur in flight of the disk or underwater; hence, dunking the opponents is allowed in order to get the Frisbee. The team with the largest score wins.

Frisbee Shuffleboard

Equipment: 8 Frisbees, 4 each color   Type: Miscellaneous—
                   Markers   special equipment

Player N: Unlimited   Area: Shallow pool

Object   To make the highest score by tossing a Frisbee at scoring markers.

Directions   Using marker lines (chairs, flags) across pool, mark off scoring area as shown below. Players toss the four Frisbees and total each set for points. After all players have tossed the frisbee, the overall total is given. Eight Frisbees allow more players to throw at one time, but total score is based on four thrown by each player.

Play may be governed by a certain amount of innings plus points *or* just total points in a time limit.

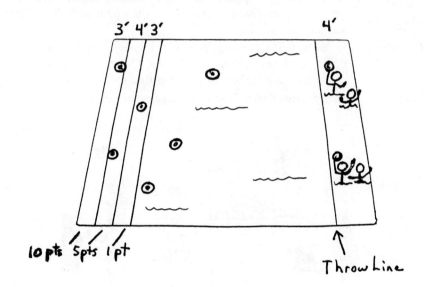

Frisbee Water Hockey

Equipment: 2 goal markers
                 Inner tube for each player
                 Frisbee
                 Team hats

Type: Miscellaneous—
           special equipment

Area: Shallow or deep pool

Player N: 2 teams of at least 6

Object   To get the Frisbee in opponents' goal.

Directions   Each team is divided in the following manner: four forwards (must travel length of pool), one goalie, and an unlimited number of guards (who cannot cross over center line). All players must be sitting in inner tubes in order to touch the Frisbee.

The Frisbee is advanced by tossing in a legal manner. All players can handle the Frisbee. A player can be dumped only if in possession of the Frisbee.

Goals count one point each; there must be at least one pass before attempt. Game is played to a time limit with the highest scoring team the winner.

Penalty   A player will sit out one minute for each of the following: (1) tipping a player without the Frisbee, (2) guard going over the center line, and (3) unnecessary roughness.

Note   Danger from flying Frisbee—keep eyes on action.

Ring the Tube

Equipment:	4 inner tubes	Type:	Miscellaneous—
	4 kickboards		special equipment
	4 diving rings or more		
	4 diving bricks and ropes	Area:	Deep pool
	Team hats		
	Guard ropes		
Player N:	2 teams of at least 8		
	(4 goalies, 2 starters,		
	4 corner people)		

Object   To throw the diving rings into the opponents' inner tubes.

Directions   Four inner tubes are anchored by weights to mark the corner areas. Inner tubes directly opposite belong to one team.

Guard ropes are arranged to make a triangle enclosing the inner tubes and goalies. A goalie guards each tube while straddling a kickboard as if riding a horse. Goalie tries to block ring tosses and then retrieves them, throwing or handing them to teammates. Only goalies are allowed in the roped-off area; they cannot leave this area.

The starters are two people from each team who are given rings and then wait in the center of the pool until a whistle sounds. They then try to throw the rings into the opposing team's inner tubes. The corner people cannot move until the whistle is blown. They then try to block and take the rings away from the other team, and assist ring transfer from goalie to starter. The first team to get all four rings into the opposing team's inner tubes wins.

Suggestions   May wish to put masks on goalies for ring retrieval.

May be played to time limit or set score.

Variation   May add additional rings.

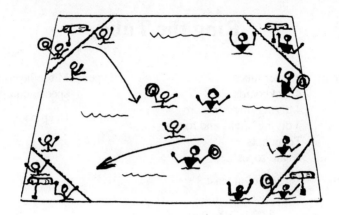

Shuffle Ring

Equipment:	1 shuffleboard cue per team	Type:	Miscellaneous—
	1 rubber ring per team		special equipment
Player N:	Unlimited	Area:	Shallow pool

Object   To complete course by pushing rubber rings underwater with shuffleboard cue before opponents.

Directions   Divide each team, half at one end of pool, half at the other end. On the command, the first player pushes the rubber ring to the other end by using the cue. The next player returns it to the opposite end until all have performed the skill. All players are waiting at their respective ends of the pool.

The first team finished is the winner.

Skittle Chip

Equipment: Kickboard   Type: Miscellaneous—special equipment

Player N: Unlimited   Area: Shallow pool

Object   To push chip onto opponents' goal area.

Directions   Kickboard ("chip") is placed in center of the pool. Players try to push the chip onto the opponents' deck. The chip may be moved only by the use of the feet, upper arms, or legs. Use of the hands and pressing the chip between the players' upper arms are not permitted.

One point is scored each time the chip hits the deck. The team with the most points wins.

Hold It Forever

Equipment:	None	Type:	Miscellaneous—underwater (relay)
Player N:	Unlimited	Area:	Shallow pool

Object   To be last team out of the water after holding breath.

Directions   All teammates except one are on the deck. On the command, the one in the water goes underwater and holds breath. As soon as that player comes up for air, the next player jumps in.

When all players have gone through breath holding, all immediately return to deck.

Last team out is the winner.

Minesweep

Equipment: 2 Diving bricks   Type: Miscellaneous—underwater

Player N: 8 or more   Area: Shallow or deep pool

Object   To move team's diving brick from one side of pool to other underwater.

Directions   Each team begins the game on the side of the pool. Two chances are allowed (i.e., two of a team's players may be used). The brick must remain underwater as shall the player(s). The brick must reach the other side in no more than two moves (or one, if a single player can go that far).

Points are scored each time the brick reaches other side. The team finishing with the most points wins.

Neat Feet

Equipment:	15–20 sinkable objects (shoes, rings, weights, etc.)	Type:	Miscellaneous—underwater
		Area:	Shallow pool

Player N: Unlimited

Object   To retrieve the largest amount of sinkable objects.

Directions   Throw all the objects into the pool. Teams begin at opposite ends of the pool. At the command, all move to the objects.

Objects are then moved back to the team's home base by use of only the feet. If an object can be carried by the toes, this is allowed.

When the object is at the side of the pool, it can then be taken with the hands and placed on the deck.

The team with the most objects wins.

Variation   Distribute half of the objects in each end of pool. Team that retrieves objects from their end of pool first wins.

Ring Retrieve

Equipment: 1 diving ring per player   Type: Miscellaneous—underwater

Player N: Unlimited   Area: Shallow pool

Object   To be the first team to retrieve all rings from pool bottom.

Directions Each team selects a ring keeper. Remaining teammates go to the opposite end of pool, find one ring, and return it to the ring keeper. Only one ring is allowed per dive. The keepers can be stationed at midpool.

The team with the most rings at the end of the time limit wins.

Variation   Play until all rings are gathered.

Wicket Cricket

Equipment:	2 medium balls	Type:	Miscellaneous—underwater
	2 basketball goals	Area:	Shallow pool
	Stopwatch		

Player N: 6 or more

Object   To be the first person to complete the circuit with the best time.

Directions   Five players are placed as wickets in the pattern shown. One player is timed by going through the legs of all the players and making a basket at each end of the course. Ball remains floating at each basket goal area. Swimmer goes through half of pattern, makes basket, and then swims through last half and makes basket. The best time wins.

Variations   Use total team times.

Use combined times of two players swimming one-half circuit each.

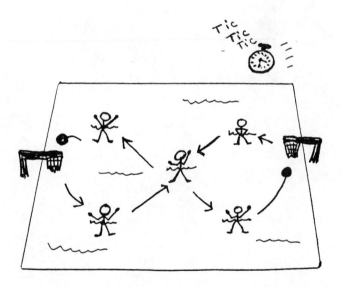

Relay

Army Ants

Equipment:	None	Type:	Relay
Player N:	Teams of 4	Area:	Shallow pool

Object   To move queen ant from one end of the pool to the other without getting her wet.

Directions   Teams of four, one designated as queen ant. Three players line up single file, queen held in laid-out position above players with head pointing in direction of movement. Players move to opposite end of pool, switching lead player by rotating to back position.

First team to complete trip wins. (Each player must be in front at least once.)

Balloon Pick-Up

Equipment: Balloon for each team   Type: Relay

Player N: Teams of 4   Area: Shallow pool

Object   To finish task first.

Directions Balloon filled with water is placed on bottom of pool before first player for each team.

Each team has half its players at opposite ends of pool.

First player must pick up balloon with feet, carry it with feet across the pool, and drop balloon to pool bottom for next swimmer to repeat process.

The first team to complete the relay wins.

74

Balloon Relay

Equipment: Balloon for each player (small size)   Type: Relay

Player N: Unlimited   Area: Shallow pool

Object   To blow up balloon, swim to opposite side, break it, and return.

Directions   Two teams of equal number compete. Each member has a balloon that is to be blown up underwater. The player then swims to the opposite side, places the balloon on the deck, and pops it. The player returns to the other side.

The first team to complete the course wins.

Variation   Each player begins with a blown-up balloon, swims on the back, and keeps the balloon in the air with light taps.

Note   Because of the balloon debris, the popping area should avoid drains, vents, gutters, etc.

Basket Crawl

Equipment: 2 basketball goals
2 balls

Player N: 5 or more per team

Type: Relay—ball

Area: Shallow or deep pool

Object To complete course by swimming and making basket before opponents.

Directions Line up baskets across pool on side deck. One player from each team will be the ball retriever.

The rest of players stand on the deck opposite basket. On the command, the first player from each team swims to the basket, is given the ball, makes a basket, and swims back. The next player jumps in and completes the process until all have gone through the course.

When the last basket is made and the player returns to stand on the deck, the ball retriever also swims over and stands on deck. The first team finished and standing on the deck wins.

Variations Change number of baskets needed to shoot.

Change strokes used.

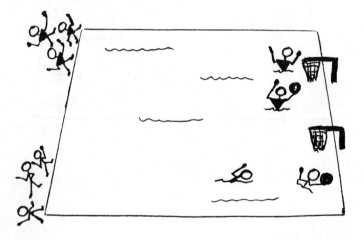

76

Basketball and Tube Relay

Equipment:	2 basketballs	Type:	Relay
	2 basketball goals	Area:	Shallow pool
	2 inner tubes		

Player N: 4 or more

Object   To be the first team to complete the course.

Directions   An inner tube and basket goal are at the opposite end of each team's course. At the signal, the first team member dives in, swims to the goal, gets into the inner tube (sitting), and attempts within five shots to make a basket.

If no shot is made, the player must go back to teammates *in* the inner tube to the next player who returns *in* the inner tube to the goal area for the same procedure.

If the shot is made, the player *leaves* the inner tube and swims back for the next player to return for a shot.

The first team to finish wins.

Basketball Relay

Equipment:	2 basketballs (Water Polo balls may be used) 2 basketball goals	Type:	Relay
		Area:	Shallow pool

Player N: Unlimited

Object   To move from one end of the pool to the other in pairs, make a basket, and return.

Directions   Two members from each team walk sideways facing each other to the opposite end of the pool. A ball is continuously passed back and forth until the players are within fifteen feet of the basket. One member shoots while the other retrieves.

When the basket is made, they return, one walking backwards, still passing the ball back and forth. The first team to finish wins.

Variations   Swim back holding the ball together between the two partners.

Have each partner make a basket before returning.

Baton Pass

Equipment:	1 baton per team	Type:	Relay—underwater
Player N:	Unlimited	Area:	Shallow pool

Object   To complete baton pass before opponents.

Directions   Two players from each team begin at opposite ends at the same time. One carries the baton. Each tries to swim underwater. If a player comes up for air, that player walks the rest of the way. After the baton exchange, each player can return to underwater swimming to other side of the pool; however, players must walk if they come up for air again. Baton is passed to the next player in line to repeat the process.

The first team finished is the winner.

Beitzel Relay

Equipment: Kickboard for each team*   Type: Relay

Player N: At least 2 teams of approximately 5   Area: Shallow pool

Object   To finish first.

Directions Set team members up as in diagram. The swimmer will maneuver the course as per diagram. Each swimmer will get thirty seconds to swim the designated style for that round. When the time limit is up, the swimmer will switch positions with one of the teammates standing in the water who hasn't gone yet.

Scoring: Points will be scored for each person the swimmer passes in the thirty seconds. The people in the water will raise their hands when the swimmer passes by and will be totaled at the end of the thirty seconds.

First round: *Run* through course

Variations Backstroke through course.

*Swim using feet only (any style kick and kickboard).

Front crawl but must swim all the way around the person before going to the next.

Blow Ball

Equipment:	1 Ping-Pong ball per team	Type:	Relay
Player N:	Unlimited	Area:	Shallow pool

Object To be the first team to complete course by blowing Ping-Pong ball along in water.

Directions Divide team, half at each end of pool. First player blows Ping-Pong ball down to other end while walking in the water. Second player blows it back. When finished each player sits on the deck.

First team finished and sitting on the deck wins.

Variations Change method of travel.

Use more than one ball.

Blue versus Red

Equipment: 15 red balloons (or more)   Type: Relay

                   15 blue balloons (or more)

                     2 inner tubes   Area: Deep pool

                     4 containers

Player N: Approximately 8 or more

Object   To get respective teams balloons from center of pool into scoring containers.

Directions   Two equally divided teams are chosen by two captains. Half of each team will be on each side of the pool.

                Captains place all balloons in center inner tubes, blues in one, reds in other. At whistle, all team members swim to center to get balloons from respective inner tube and place in scoring container placed on sides of pool. When all balloons are gone, game is over.

Scoring   Broken balloons count minus 2, whole balloons count plus 1. Team with most points wins.

Variation   May use colored balls and use a time limit instead of broken or whole balloons for winner.

Carrying Relays

Equipment:	Special gear for each type of race	Type:	Relay
		Area:	Shallow or deep pool
Player N:	Teams of 4 or more		

Object   To complete task first.

Directions   *Waiter race:* Swimmer carries paper plate with cup on it filled with water, using scissors kick and shallow arm pull.

Teaspoon-ball: Swimmer carries a Ping-Pong ball in a teaspoon to next swimmer.

Rainy Day: Swimmer carries opened umbrella across pool to next swimmer.

Whistle while you work: Swimmer carries two soda crackers across pool, gets out, eats crackers and whistles stanza of selected song, then returns.

Note: The cracker/whistle portion is great fun! (Author's Note)

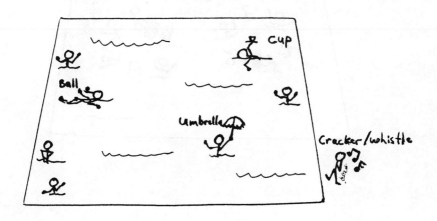

Circle Up

Equipment: 1 diving brick per team   Type: Relay

Player N: Unlimited   Area: Shallow or deep pool

Object   To complete number of circles with brick before opponents.

Directions   Form a circle for each team with all team players. On the command, the brick is passed from player to player the stated number of times. First team finished is the winner.

Penalty   If the brick is dropped the count starts over.

Variations   Change the size of the circle; change the number of revolutions.

Put blindfolds on each player necessitating the use of names to find each person in the succession of passes.

Combination Relay

Equipment: 1 for each team: kickboard, pullbuoy, inner tube
Swim fins

Type: Relay

Area: Shallow pool

Player N: Unlimited

Object To finish combination course before other team.

Directions Divide the teams as per the diagram. All members must begin on the deck. Numbers one and two use kickboards and inner tubes, numbers three and four use leg floats and arms only. Numbers five and six use swim fins.

Each team member must wait on the deck until the preceding player completes the lap.

The first team finished with all players on the deck is the winner.

Combination Swim

Equipment:	1 diving brick per team	Type:	Relay
Player N:	Unlimited	Area:	Shallow pool

Object

To complete swim course with diving brick and prescribed strokes.

Directions

First team member swims length carrying brick above the water with either the elementary backstroke or sidestroke and leaves the brick on the deck. Return stroke is the corkscrew (alternating front and back crawl). The second team member swims corkscrew down, picks up the brick, and returns with same procedure as number one's initial lap.

The changing of procedures continues with all team members until all have completed the course.

The first team to complete the course is the winner.

Conditioning Swim

Equipment:	None	Type:	Relay
Player N:	2 teams of at least 4	Area:	Shallow and deep pool

Object   To be first team to finish drill.

Directions   Members of each team dive into shallow pool end, swim length, and get out. They then climb up to high dive platform, jump off, swim length, get out, and tag teammate who repeats action.

First team finished is the winner.

Variation   May predetermine specific strokes to be used.

Note   This <u>may</u> have to be adapted to your pool situation.

Crab Walk Relay

Equipment:	2 10-pound weight belts	Type:	Relay—special equipment

Player N:	Unlimited	Area:	Shallow pool

Object   To complete crab relay before other team.

Directions   Place half of each team on each side of the pool. On the command, one member submerges with weight belt placed on stomach and proceeds to walk in crab* fashion across bottom of pool.

*The crab walk is done on the back with hands and feet on the bottom. The player may come up at any time for air. The first team finished is the winner.

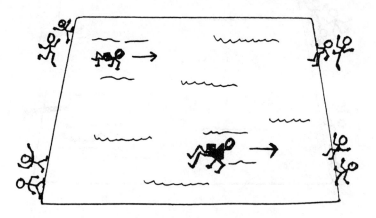

Cross-Water Relay

Equipment:	None	Type:	Relay
Player N:	2 teams of 6	Area:	Shallow

Object   To be team to finish first.

Directions   One player from each team is sent across width of pool to stand on the second line from that edge with legs apart. Rest of team is lined up.

Each player dog-paddles across width of pool, swimming between legs of teammates on way over. Swimmer executes four front-back layouts, swims between the legs of teammate, and crawls to beginning station. Front-back layouts refer to player floating prone (front) and then floating back (supine) and flipping back and forth to each.

Next player must be touched on the hand before beginning the sequence.

Variations Continue sequence two or three times.

Crawl stroke over, swim through the legs, and hop back with hands out of the water.

Breaststroke over, swim through the legs, and corkscrew stroke to return.

89

Deep Six

Equipment: 2 or more diving bricks   Type: Relay—underwater

Player N: Unlimited   Area: Deep pool

Object   To be first team to complete brick retrieve and drop.

Directions   Divide teams evenly. A diving brick is placed at the bottom of the pool. Each team member must start on the deck, dive and retrieve brick, and drop it again for the next player. First team to finish is the winner.

Dive and Go Seek

Equipment: Enough diving weights for each player or 12 per team—2 colors
Receptacle for each team (basket)

Type: Relay—underwater

Area: Deep pool

Player N: 2 teams of at least 4

Object   For each team to retrieve all the objects of one color from the bottom of the pool and to place them in the appropriate container at the side of the pool.

Directions   To begin, the teams are both in the water on opposite sides of the pool. The colored diving objects are tossed at random into the pool.

At the whistle, both teams begin to find and retrieve the objects, one at a time, and place them in the container at their side of the pool. The first team to retrieve all of their colored objects is the winner.

Best two out of three contests is the team winner.

Rules and Penalties   Referee will make certain no more than one object is retrieved at a time. Failure to comply will result in all team's objects being tossed back into the pool, plus an additional weight.

Dog-Paddle Relay

Equipment:	4 medium balls , one per team	Type:	Relay
	4 hats (different colors for each team)	Area:	Shallow pool

Player N: 4 per team

Object   To complete course by pushing the ball with head and moving by use of the dog paddle.

Directions One player with a ball is placed in each corner of the pool. From the starting point, the first player dog-paddles, pushing the ball only with his or her head, to the next corner and stops. The next player goes to the next corner, and so on for all members.

He When the final member reaches the starting corner, all on the team jump out of the pool and the relay is finished.

Variations If less than four players per team, players can swim a greater distance.

Add barking to movement.

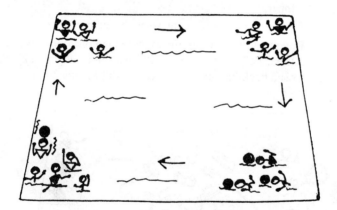

Dolphin Relay

Equipment:	1 diving brick per team	Type:	Relay
Player N:	Unlimited	Area:	Shallow pool

Object — To complete course by using the dolphin kick and dive throughout relay.

Directions — The first player performs the dolphin kick while swimming underwater across the pool. During the swim the diving brick is dropped from the player's hand. The second leg of the relay leaves from the opposite side of the pool at the same time as the first, and performs the dolphin dive searching for the brick. When found, swimmer carries it across pool to next player.

When all have completed the swim, the relay is over and the first team finished is the winner.

Donut Diving Relay

Equipment:	4 diving rings	Type:	Relay—underwater
Player N:	2 teams of at least 3	Area:	Shallow and deep pool

Object   To swim across pool, drop diving rings, recover opponents' diving rings, and swim back to starting point.

Directions   The first member of each team starts from the shallow end of the pool in the water, carrying one diving ring in each hand. Swimmer must use either breaststroke or sidestroke.

After reaching the deep end of the pool, the swimmer drops one diving ring approximately twenty feet from the end and the second diving ring at the end.

The swimmer now crosses to the opposite side of the pool and collects the diving rings dropped by the opposing team and swims with them back to team. The rings are then passed to the next member who repeats the procedure.

If the opposing swimmer reaches the spot before a ring has been dropped, both rings must be dropped immediately. (This would allow the retriever to catch them before they touch the bottom.)

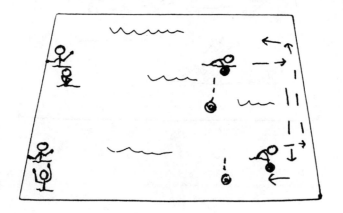

Equipment Relay

Equipment: 2 hand paddles per team   Type: Relay
                 2 swim fins per team
                                           Area: Shallow pool

Player N: 4 per team

Object   To swim and collect all equipment before other team.

Directions Place the four pieces of equipment at one end of the pool. The teams should assemble at the other end.

On the command, the first player from each team swims down and gets one hand paddle, puts it on, returns, and gives it to the next player. This process is continued through the fins.

The first team with all the equipment wins.

95

Exchange Relay

Equipment: 2 diving rings per team   Type: Relay
                 2 pullbuoys per team
                                          Area: Shallow pool

Player N: Teams of 2

Object   To be first to complete task.

Directions   Teams start at end or side of pool. First person swims length or
width, underwater, with a diving ring in each hand. Player
leaves the rings at opposite side, grabs two pullbuoys, and
swims back to start. Teammate then takes two pullbuoys to opposite side, picks up two diving rings, and returns underwater
with them to beginning point.

The first team finished is the winner.

Get the Lead Out

Equipment:	2 5- or 10-pound weight belts	Type:	Relay—underwater
Player N:	Unlimited	Area:	Deep pool

Object   To be first to complete task.

Directions Place belts at bottom of deep pool. Each member of the team must surface dive into the pool, retrieve belt, hold above water, call out entire name, and then drop belt for next team member.

The first team finished is the winner.

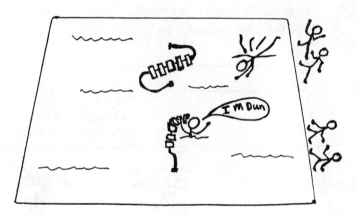

97

Hail the Brick

Equipment: 1 diving brick per team   Type: Relay

Player N: Unlimited   Area: Shallow or deep pool

Object   To complete the course in couples, carrying a brick.

Directions Players work in pairs. The diving brick is to be carried out of the
water by the two players to the opposite side/end of the pool and
back.

Each couple tries to complete the course swimming one stroke,
keeping the brick out of the water. The brick should be carried
by the inside hand of each couple.

The first team finished is the winner.

Head and Foot

Equipment:	2 soccer balls	Type:	Relay
Player N:	Unlimited	Area:	Shallow or deep pool

Object   To push ball from one side to the other before the other team.

Directions   Teams are divided, half on one side, half on the other. All are out of the water to begin. First member of each team jumps in the water and pushes the ball across the pool using the head. Any movement can be used. The second team member pushes it back again using the feet.

The first team to finish alternating between the head and feet is the winner.

Hilarity Plus Relay

Equipment: 2 large sweatshirts
2 chairs
2 umbrellas
2 whistles
2 pairs tennis shoes

Type: Relay—special equipment

Area: Deep pool

Player N: 6 or more

Object To complete obstacle course before other team.

Directions Place the chairs, umbrellas, and whistles at the opposite end of the deep pool.

The first team member of each group puts on tennis shoes and sweatshirt. On the signal, both jump or dive into the water and swim to other side.

The following is then performed: (1) sit in chair, (2) pick up umbrella and whistle, and (3) open umbrella while continually blowing whistle. The player then does five each of toe touches, sit-ups, and jumping jacks and goes to the diving board for the return swim. The next teammate must put same outfit on and complete the same routine.

First team finished is the winner.

Variations Use flippers in place of shoes. Have person sing familiar song rather than blow whistle.

Travel in inner tubes instead of swimming.

Change number and/or kind of exercises.

Note This is a very funny relay! (Author's note)

Holding Hands Relay

Equipment: None   Type: Relay

Player N: 2 teams of 3 or more   Area: Shallow pool

Object   To be the first team to complete the exercise.

Directions Player 1 runs across pool and swims back to starting point. Player 1 and player 2 hold hands, run across pool, and swim back to a starting point. Players 1, 2, and 3 hold hands, run across pool, and swim back to starting point.

This is continued until entire team completes task as a unit.

Variation Players swim both ways.

In and Out the Windows

Equipment:	Inner tube for each player	Type:	Relay
	2 pullbuoys per team	Area:	Shallow pool
Player N:	Teams of 2		

Object   To be first to complete task.

Directions Teams must stand at sides of pool, touching the wall. Players push their inner tubes toward the middle of the pool then return to wall. Players then lock hands or wrists and swim to the tubes and through them, one at a time, keeping the hands clasped; they then must continue to the end of the pool, pick up two pullbuoys, and swim back to the start.

The first team to finish wins.

Inner Tube Relay Race

Equipment:	1 inner tube per team	Type:	Relay
Player N:	4 per team	Area:	Shallow pool

Object   To complete inner tube relay before other team.

Directions Each team has two players at one end of the pool and two at the opposite end. Players 1 and 3 propel the inner tube only with the hands, while players 2 and 4 use only the feet.

Hands or feet must be in contact with the inner tube at all times depending on which part the player is using. The first team finished is the winner.

Variations Use one hand and one foot.

Swim with inner tube over body.

Knee Ball

Equipment:	4 medium balls	Type:	Relay
Player N:	12 or more	Area:	Shallow pool

Object   To be the first team to complete the course carrying the ball between the knees.

Directions   Each team member walks or jumps from one end of pool to the other carrying the ball between the knees. The first team to finish is the winner.

Variations   Change the method of movement.

Change the size of the ball.

Lit Candle Relay

Equipment:	Long candle for each team Spare candles and matches	Type:	Relay
Player N:	At least 6 per team	Area:	Shallow pool for non-swimmers Deep pool for swimmers

Object To be first team to successfully finish relay.

Directions The first team member carries lit candle to next team member using any swim skill (or walking). This procedure is repeated until all team members have carried the lit candle.

Suggestion Judges should have extra candles ready.

Length that candle is carried by team members may be varied according to skills.

Monday Washday

Equipment:	4 washcloths per team	Type:	Relay
	4 towels per team		
	4 clothespins per team	Area:	Deep pool
	1 long clothes line		

| Player N: | Teams of 4 |

Object   To complete task first.

Directions Swimmer carries articles across pool using sidestroke and clips them to line. Returns to team with crawl.

Second swimmer crawls to line and removes articles; swims then to next player using sidestroke. First team to finish is the winner.

No Hands!

Equipment: Ball for each team   Type: Relay

Player N: Teams of 4   Area: Shallow or deep pool

Object   To be first team to complete task.

Directions   Teams are divided, half on one side, half on the other. The first player pushes ball across pool with breaststroke kick while holding hands behind back. The next player returns ball to other side of pool in same manner.

First team to finish is the winner.

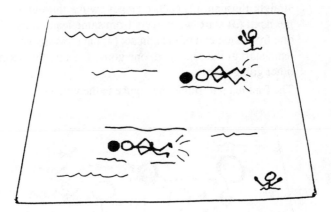

Obstacle Course Relay

Equipment: 5 hula hoops per team
5 weights per team
5 ropes per team

Type: Relay—special equipment

Area: Shallow pool

Player N: Unlimited

Object To complete the course before the opposing team does.

Directions Arrange hula hoops at varying depths by attaching different lengths of rope (string) to the weights and then to the hoops. The hoops should float up to the surface.

The course can be done in several ways: (1) each member swims straight through; (2) each member swims through one and over the next; (3) start two players from same team at the same time, one from each end of the course; (4) have two players from same team start at the same end, one going through the hoops and the other going over.

The first team to finish the course is the winner.

Over/Under Relay

Equipment:	None	Type:	Relay
Player N:	2 teams of at least 5	Area:	Shallow or deep pool

Object To finish first.

Directions Each team is lined up single file. Swimmer 1 begins *over* next person in line and *under* the second person and so on until the end of the line is reached and calls to the next person to begin.

Swimmer 2 begins *over* and then *under*, etc.

Each swimmer follows same format (always starting *over*) until all have completed the course and swim to side of pool designating completion of the race.

Note When performed in deep water, presents excellent treading exercise.

Variations Tunnel swim through outstretched legs of teammates only.

Leapfrog over teammates only.

Partner Parody

Equipment: None   Type: Relay

Player N: At least 12   Area: Deep pool

Object   To perform the same skill as partner—jump or dive—on command, without communicating in any way.

Directions   Each team divides in half and lines up on opposite sides of pool. At the whistle or command, the first person in each group will either jump or dive into water. If they both performed *same* skill, they may sit on side. If they performed *opposite* skills, they must go to end of line and repeat.

Team sitting first wins.

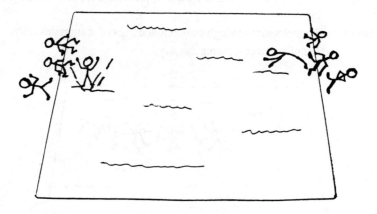

Pass the Jug

Equipment: 2 plastic bottles with handles   Type: Relay
(bleach bottles)

Area: Shallow pool

Player N: Unlimited

Object   To move the bottle from one end of the line to the other.

Directions   Captains are chosen, who in turn choose teams, alternating male, female choices. Teams line up across the pool about three feet apart with captain at the end. The bottle is passed under the legs of each member until it reaches the end of the line. The captain will swim freestyle with the bottle to the head of the line. The first captain to come to the start of the line wins for his or her team.

Variation   Each member can swim up to the front when bottle reaches the end. When the players are back in their original places, game is over.

Pull and Glide

Equipment:	None	Type:	Relay
Player N:	Unlimited	Area:	Shallow pool

Object   To complete course by pulling teammate through water before opponents.

Directions   Divide into teams and then into couples. One player walking backward will pull partner in back float position to the opposite end of the pool. Players then switch places and return. This process is done by all team members until all players have completed the course.

The first team finished is the winner.

Variations   Push floating partner hand-to-hand while arms are kept straight.

Both players on back. First player pulls on ankles of partner as they move to opposite end of pool.

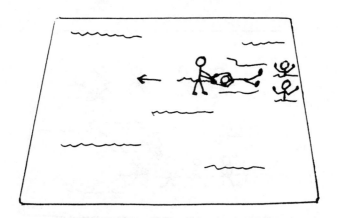

Pullbuoy Basketball Relay

Equipment:	2 pullbuoys per team	Type:	Relay
	1 ball per team	Area:	Shallow pool
	1 basketball goal		

Player N: Teams of 2

Object   To be first to complete task.

Directions   First team member puts the pullbuoys on hands, swims across the width of the pool, pushing a ball ahead. Player must make a basket, return, and give the buoys and ball to teammate who repeats action.

First team to finish wins.

Push 'Em

Equipment:	Kickboard and pullbuoy per team	Type:	Relay
Player N:	Teams of 2	Area:	Shallow pool

Object   To be first to complete task.

Directions   Teams start at end or side of pool. First player extends kickboard in front and has pullbuoy gripped between knees. Partner pushes floating player at feet or ankles the length or width of pool. Team members switch places and repeat.

First team to finish wins.

Pushblock

Equipment:	1 10-pound diving brick per team	Type:	Relay
Player N:	4 per team	Area:	Shallow pool

Object   To complete brick push course before the other team.

Directions   Each team consists of two couples. On the command, two players from each team begin to push the brick to their teammates at the opposite end of the pool.

One player is pushing underwater, the other does the breaststroke beside that player. When the pusher comes up for air, the surface player goes down to continue the push.

This procedure continues to the opposite end where the other team members return the brick in the same manner.

The brick must remain in contact with the pool bottom. The first team to complete the relay wins.

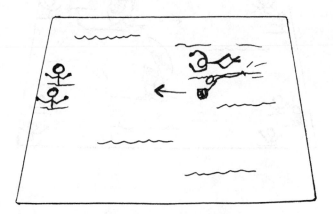

Reading Relay

Equipment:	Newspaper or magazine for each team	Type:	Relay
Player N:	At least 6 per team	Area:	Shallow pool for nonswimmers Deep pool for swimmers

Object   To be first team to successfully finish relay.

Directions   The first team member swims on back (or walks), reading article loudly, and then transfers both tasks to next team member at opposite end of pool.

The first team to complete the relay wins.

116

Shoe Swim

Equipment: 1 pair of tennis shoes per player   Type: Relay—underwater

Player N: Unlimited   Area: Shallow pool

Object   To retrieve each player's shoes, put on feet, and swim back to starting point.

Directions   Place each team's shoes underwater at the opposite end of the shallow pool in a pile. Shoes should be marked in some manner so that each player can find own shoes. On the command of "go," everyone swims to the designated shoe pile, finds own shoes, places on feet, ties shoelaces, and swims back to the starting point.

When the entire team is sitting on the side of the pool, game is over.

Siamese Twins

Equipment:	Leg ties for each couple	Type:	Relay
Player N:	12 or more	Area:	Shallow pool

Object To get all team members to opposite end of pool before other team.

Directions Divide each team into pairs and tie each pair's inside legs together. On the command, the first pair jumps in and swims (any stroke) to the opposite end of the pool, gets out, and sits on the deck. The next pair follows when the first completes the course, and so on until all have gone.

If either player in a pair touches bottom of pool, the pair must start over.

The first team sitting on the opposite deck is the winner.

Soggy Sweatshirt Relay

Equipment:	Large, long-sleeved sweatshirt for each team	Type:	Relay
Player N:	At least 6 per team	Area:	Shallow pool for nonswimmers Deep pool for swimmers

Object   To be first team to successfully finish relay.

Directions   The first player on each team puts on wet shirt, jumps or dives into pool, swims or walks across, takes off shirt in water, and hands to next team member. Play continues until all team members have completed task.

First team to finish wins.

Variation   Add sweatpants, bathing caps, etc.
May get out of pool before removing shirt.

Squeeze the Orange

Equipment: 2 or more oranges   Type: Relay

Player N: Unlimited   Area: Shallow pool

Directions   Line up players, one behind the other. Each team is given an orange. The orange is passed from player to player by the chin. No hands are allowed. If the orange is dropped, it is taken back to the head of the line.

First team to complete the passing of the orange is the winner.

Variation   Arrange in shuttle (half of team on each side of pool); each person swims with ball or orange under chin to other group.

120

Stack and Go

Equipment:	3 inner tubes per team	Type:	Relay
Player N:	Multiples of 3	Area:	Shallow pool

Object To be the first team to complete the course using three inner tubes and three players per set or length.

Directions Stack three inner tubes on top of each other. One teammate gets on top of the stack. Two other players swim or walk the stack to the opposite end of the pool where the next set takes a turn.

The first team to complete the course is the winner.

Stacked Deck

Equipment:	8 kickboards	Type:	Relay—special equipment
Player N:	8 or more	Area:	Shallow pool

Object   To complete course carrying the total number of kickboards required.

Directions   Four team members are standing at one end of the pool. Four kickboards are stacked on the other end.

At the command, one member swims to the boards, picks up one and swims back, giving it to the next person in line. The next person swims with the board to the other end, picks up a second board and returns with two boards to the third person in line. Play continues until all boards are retrieved.

Any stroke can be used.

Variation   Specify type of stroke.

Tandem Stroking

Equipment:	None	Type:	Relay
Player N:	Teams of 2	Area:	Shallow or deep pool

Object To complete task first.

Directions Players work in pairs. First swimmer uses front crawl arm stroke to cross pool while second swimmer holds feet of first swimmer and uses flutter kick to aid in crossing pool. They trade positions and strokes and return to beginning.

The first team to complete the course wins.

Variations Back crawl or elementary backstroke (first swimmer hooks feet under armpits of second swimmer).

Sidestroke (second swimmer holding feet of first swimmer with one hand).

Crawl tandem with three or more swimmers.

Team Obstacles

Equipment: Inner tube for each player
Ball for each team

Type: Relay
Area: Shallow pool

Player N: Teams of 2

Object   To be first to complete task.

Directions   Teams sit in inner tubes and fold arms across chest. Players must then push a ball with the inner tube the length or width of the pool and back (while sitting in the inner tubes), kicking with the feet and *not* using hands.

Variation   Players may *not* kick with their feet. All forward momentum must be obtained by use of the hands. Using just the hands to paddle, the players move the ball down the length or width and back, pushing it with the inner tube.

Three Arm–Three Leg Race

Equipment: Ties (material to join arms and legs)   Type: Relay

Player N: Unlimited pairs   Area: Shallow pool

Object   To complete course with legs or arms tied with partners.

Directions   Pair up in twos and then in teams, if desired. Tie one set of arms and one set of legs together. Pairs try to reach other end to win, using any method of travel.

Variations   May tie arms only or legs only.

Players not allowed to touch bottom.

Tube and Fin

Equipment:	4 inner tubes per team	Type:	Relay
	2 hand paddles per team		
	2 fins per team	Area:	Shallow pool
	1 face mask per team		

Player N: 4 or more

Object   To complete course from one end to other before other team.

Directions One player from each team wears the following: four inner tubes around waist, hand paddles on each hand, fins on each foot, and a face mask (on face!).

On the command, the first player from each team leaps into the water and swims to the other end on their backs. At that point, each player removes two inner tubes, sits on them, and returns. Players remove all equipment and give to next team members, who repeat process.

Each player must remain on the tubes to complete the relay.

The first team to successfully complete the relay wins.

Tube Basketball Relay

Equipment: 2 inner tubes
                 2 balls
                 2 basketball goals

Type: Relay

Area: Shallow or deep pool

Player N: 2 teams of 3 or more

Object   To be the first team to complete task.

Directions   One player from each team sits in inner tubes. The ball is placed on lap or between knees. Player must paddle to the hoop, shoot the ball into the hoop, retrieve ball, return to the starting side of the pool, and pass ball to next player.

The first team to finish wins.

Tube Twist

Equipment:	1 inner tube per team	Type:	Relay
Player N:	4 per team	Area:	Shallow pool

Object To be the first team to complete the course.

Directions Each team consists of four players: three in the water holding the inner tube and one on the deck.

At the signal, the deck player dives into the water and comes up in the middle of the inner tube. The center player pushes the inner tube ahead while walking on the pool floor.

The outside players must continually rotate the tube around the center player while still moving in a forward pattern (walking).

The first team to reach the finish line is the winner.

Variations Players may swim in place of walking.

Can be played in deep pool.

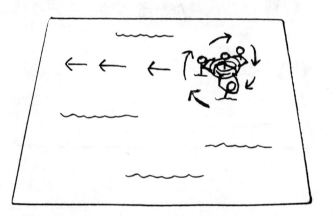

Volleyball Relay

Equipment: 2 or more volleyballs or similar balls   Type: Relay

Player N: At least 4 per team   Area: Shallow pool

Object   To complete relay by carrying ball between knees.

Directions   Divide teams in half. The first members of each team begin in the water. Using crawl arms only, the player swims the length of the pool, keeping the ball between the knees. Ball is given to teammate who returns to other side of pool in the same manner. The game is over when all team members have completed the run. The first team to finish is the winner.

Variation   The type of stroke can vary: back crawl, breaststroke, etc.

Water Brick Relay

Equipment:	1 diving brick per team	Type:	Relay
Player N:	Unlimited	Area:	Deep pool

Object To complete brick pass before opponents.

Directions Have team line up, one behind the other. On the command, the first person passes the brick between legs to next player, who passes it over the head to the next and so on. When the brick reaches the end, all players turn around and return the brick in the same manner. All must tread water the whole time.

The first team finished by placing the brick on the side is the winner.

Tag

Chinese (Water) Checkers Game

Equipment: Kickboard for each player   Type: Tag

Player N: 2 teams of at least 4   Area: Shallow or deep pool

Object   Be the first team to get all members against the opponents' (opposite) pool side.

Directions   Players move by sitting in an upright manner upon the kickboard. Movement may be done individually or as a group to the other side of the pool, trying to hinder opponents' movement. This is done by knocking the members of the opposing side off their boards.

Rules   No human chains or walls may be made.

   Team members may assist team members in danger.

   No pulling of hair or suit.

   No kicking—use hands and body only.

   Boards may not be used to flip opponent.

   A person losing kickboard or turned upside down and unable to get upright must return to line near wall and start over. Player may get back to this line by any method but may *not* enter into play.

Suggestion   Plan some method so that slower or poorer swimmers are protected to better their chance of reaching other side.

Freeze It

Equipment:	3 medium balls	Type:	Tag—ball
Player N:	10 or more	Area:	Shallow pool

Object   To be the last person to be frozen.

Directions   Three players are chosen as "It." These players try to hit the free players with one of the balls. If a free player is hit outright or with a floating ball, that player must freeze. Only another free player can unfreeze the player that is frozen, by touching that player with their hand. A free player may go underwater to avoid being tagged.

The last free player is the winner.

"Jaws"

Equipment:	None	Type:	Tag
Player N:	Unlimited	Area:	Deep pool

Object To elude tag and be remaining free player.

Directions Choose one shark who continually treads water in the middle of the deep pool. All other players (minnows) line up on one side of the pool.

The shark, with back to the minnows, calls out "shark." All players have ten seconds to jump in and swim to the other side in any manner possible without being tagged.

If tagged before reaching safety, that player becomes a shark. Calls continue until only one player remains a minnow.

The last player free is the winner and can become the new shark.

Note This game has also been called "Sharks and Minnows."

Paddleboard Tag

Equipment:	Medium ball	Type:	Tag—special equipment
	Kickboard for each player	Area:	Deep pool
Player N:	Unlimited		

Object To put other players out by hitting any part of the body with the ball.

Directions All players have a kickboard in the deep pool. Only the kickboard can block a thrown ball. If the ball hits a player's body on the fly or bounce, that player is out.

If the ball goes out of the pool, eliminated players may throw it back in and return to the game if a player is hit with it.

Play continues until one player remains.

Penalty If the ball is blocked with the hands, that player must get out and wait for a ball that lands outside the pool for a return opportunity.

Prison Inner Tube Ball

Equipment: Inner tube for each player
                   3 balls

Player N: 2 teams of at least 4

Type: Tag—prison ball

Area: Shallow or deep pool
          (divide into half pool
          and prisons)

Object   To win the game, all of the opponents must be put in prison.

Directions Everyone sits in inner tube. A team may not cross the half line or go into the other team's prison to get a ball. Three balls are played at the same time.

To put opponents in prison, they must be hit anywhere on the body with the ball except upon the head. If player touches a ball when it is thrown, that player is still eligible for play.

To get out of prison, a prisoner must hit someone on the opposing team with the ball (except on head).

136

Pssst!

Equipment: 1 pair taped swim goggles   Type: Tag

Player N: Unlimited   Area: Shallow or deep pool

Object   To try and tag new players who become the blindman.

Directions   All players tread water in deep pool or stand without motion in shallow pool (if used). One player is chosen as the blindman and wears the taped goggles.

Play begins with the blindman in the center of the pool. All players must verbally say "Pssst" in order that the blindman can catch another player who then becomes the blindman.

A time limit can be used to control the game.

Pursuit

Equipment:	None	Type:	Tag
Player N:	Unlimited	Area:	Shallow or deep pool

Object   To tag a free player.

Directions   Pairs of players station themselves throughout the pool standing together. One pursuer and one pursuee are chosen to play. These two players must be in continual motion at all times. In order not to be tagged, the pursuee can link with one of the pairs. The remaining partner becomes the new pursuer.

Variation   Make more than one set of pursuers and pursuees.

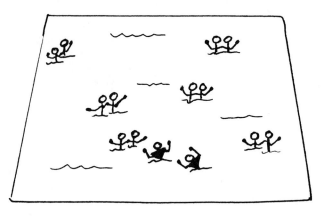

Save the Whales

Equipment: 4 kickboards   Type: Tag
                  6 elastic arm bands
                                        Area: Shallow or deep pool

Player N: 10 pr more as follows:
                  6 whales
                  2 scouts (for killer ship)
                  2 scouts (for Greenpeace)

Object   Whales try to remain free; killer scouts try to tag whales; peace scouts set whales free by removing the tags.

Directions   Game is begun when all scouts have kickboards and whales are assigned to pods (groups) of two. Scouts of both kinds must trap whales by remaining at all times on the surface.

Whales may use main advantage of surface dive to escape killers and peace scouts. Scouts may corner whales for the catch.

Killers must place an elastic band on one of the two whales in a pod to score. Peace scouts score by collecting the tags. The game *begins* with the killers having three tags and three whales already tagged.

The game is played for a five-minute time limit. Change so all play different positions. The team with the most tags on the whales (killers) or collected (peace) wins.

Walking Amoeba

Equipment: None   Type: Tag

Player N: Unlimited   Area: Shallow pool

Object   To catch all players by touching or trapping them.

Directions Two players are selected as the "Amoeba." All other players
are called "photoplankton." These players spread out over the
entire pool.

The two players forming the amoeba join hands and try to capture the other players. If a player is trapped, that player joins
hands with the others and becomes a part of the amoeba. Players
may escape by swimming over or under amoeba.

Game is over when only three photoplankton are free from the
hungry amoeba.

WaterPlay Contributions

If you would like to share one of your WaterPlay creations with others or report a variation to one in this book, please fill out the following form and mail to:

Dr. Mary Ann Humphrey, Coordinator, Physical Education and Health
Portland Community College, Rock Creek Campus
Box 19000
Portland, Oregon 97219-0990

Title   Type:

Equipment: Area:

Player N:

Object:

Directions:

Rules:

Penalties:

Variations:

Diagram